What They're Saying About This Book

"Your conviction (and your writing ability) brings great clarity to ideas. The book reads like magic."

—The New City Library

"A fine job. I can see the book with its clear, no-nonsense message being used by many groups."

—Catherine Hubbell, Editor "Creative Thought" magazine

"Your material is new and different. It is good."

—Dr. Raymond Charles Barker, Minister, First Church of Religious Science, N.Y.C.

"The work is enriched with a style, easy to follow, that we find it pleasant to just continue after we have started. And I can assure you that as you read the book, you will listen to the gentle stirrings of God's grace in your heart. It is a useful overview of the whole matter of life and a worthwhile book to have in your library."

—Commonweal

"It s fundamental message is so powerful."

—Mind Expander, newsletter of the Phenix Society

"Kenneth Thurston Hurst is one of those unique individuals who combines both spirituality and business in his life in such a way that both are enriched by his contributions to writing, living and lecturing. He exemplifies how to apply spiritual principles in today's modern world."

—Rev. Elizabeth Wall Fenske, President-Emeritus, Spiritual Frontiers Fellowship

"This books uniqueness consists of the concise clarity of what is said and the magnificent demonstration of the author's application to these principles in his own life. It is an excellent book of its kind, and any willing to make the effort can really put a light into their lives by putting to work the simple, practical exercises he recommends. *Highly recommended!''*

—Charles C. Wise, Jr., Spiritual Frontiers Journal

"A most insightful 'self-help' book along the lines of The Power of Positive Thinking. The concepts of the book are practical and easily incorporated into daily life."

—The Beacon

LIVE LIFE FIRST CLASS!

LIVE LIFE FIRST CLASS!

HOW TO BE HAPPIER, HEALTHIER, AND MORE PROSPEROUS...

Kenneth Thurston Hurst

a **M**ountainvue PUBLICATION

Second Printing, 1987

Distributed by
Larson Publications
4936 Route 414
Burdett, N.Y. 14818

ISBN 0-943914-45-0

Library of Congress Cataloging in Publication Data

Hurst, Kenneth Thurston, 1923–
   Live life first class!

   Bibliography: p.
   1. Success. 2. New Thought. I. Title.
BJ1611.2.H87 1985   158'.1   85–3230
ISBN 0-943914-45-0

Typeset in 11 point Times Roman
Printed in the United States by
Mitchell-Shear, Inc.
Ann Arbor, MI

Contents

Life is a dream,
a little more coherent than most.

—Pascal

To P.B. . . . always

I have a neighbor, Ed Geller, who stops in from time to time.

He happened to come around when I was reviewing the galley proofs of this book. Naturally, he asked what it was about. I told him. He listened carefully. Then he said, "What you mean is, if you live right, God returns the kindness."

"Ed!" I exclaimed, "You've summed up in one sentence what I've taken a whole book to explain! "

So that's why I've put Ed's statement right up front.

Prologue

Let me tell you how I got the title for this book *Live Life First Class!* I had been vacationing in Switzerland and when the time came to leave, I took a taxi to the station to catch a train to Geneva whence I would fly back to New York. Upon arriving at the station a porter took my suitcases and asked me, "Are you traveling first class or second class?"

"First class," I replied.

He led me down the platform and said, "Stand right here. This is where the first class compartment of the train will stop."

"How do you know that?" I asked. "Do they stop in the same places every time?"

"No, they stop at different places. But it's my job to know where the different compartments for each train stop."

Sitting in the train enroute to Geneva I thought to myself, life is something like that.

First, you have to figure out where the train compartment stops, and if you want to travel first class, where that compartment stops. Then you have to position yourself for it. It doesn't take very much effort to do so, but you have to make that slight effort.

And to live life truly first class does not require all that much extra effort. It requires a small effort admittedly. But anyone can do it.

In the business world we used to say that successful executives do not have to be twice as smart as their peers. No, they only have to be ten percent more intelligent, have ten percent more drive and ten percent more ambition. Then they would be in the top executive echelons. That's all, only ten percent more.

And so with life. Leading a life based on the principles outlined in this book does not require twice as much effort, only about ten percent more effort. And it becomes easier as you go along. You become accustomed to it, to thinking in a certain way, to disciplining yourself to behave in the correct manner. You learn how to RE-NEW your life "through the transforming of your mind," as St. Paul pointed out.

And the rewards are so worth it! It's the difference between day and night, between enduring a ho-hum existence or truly living a sublime adventure.

Henry David Thoreau said most people live lives of quiet desperation. This book will show you how to rise above the rest, how to lead a happier, healthier and more prosperous life, how to truly live life first class!

CHAPTER I

What this Book Will Do for You

This book shows you in simple, easy-to-understand language exactly *what* to do and *how* to do it to get the most out of life. You learn easy-to-use techniques anybody can apply *immediately* in everyday life.

It occurred to me one day that at school they teach us reading, writing and 'rithmetic, but they don't teach us anything about the most important subject of all—*how to live.* Because what good are all the other subjects if the most important of all—living itself—is ignored? We cannot escape from the daily business of living. That's what it's all about. But no one tells us how to tackle the job of living, no school teacher instructs us in the art of successful living. So generation after generation is flung into the world completely unprepared to cope with it. Except those few who seem to enjoy the best life has to offer. Why is it some people are more successful than others? Happier? More prosperous? Obviously they have mastered the art of living. And there *is* an art to living. Like any worthwhile sport or hobby it requires first learning the ground rules, and then applying them. It's that simple.

If you wanted to take up golf, for instance, you wouldn't just buy a set of golf clubs and hie off to the nearest course, and start walloping away at the ball. No, first you read a book or two on golf to learn what it's all about, to study the rules. Then you take lessons from a golf pro, and then you practice and practice at a golf range until you feel competent to take your place on the links in company with others.

Or consider the game of bridge. You'd be very unpopular if you tried to make up a foursome without knowing anything about the game. You'd only spoil your partner's enjoyment. As with golf, you have to learn the rules, then put them into practice until they become second nature.

Successful living is like learning to drive a car. In the old days when we had stick-shifts, remember learning to engage gears? One . . . clutch . . . two, etc. And remember how you clashed gears frequently, making an awful grinding sound? But you soon learned to change gears smoothly and before long it became second nature and you no longer had to concentrate on what you were doing.

Same with the best and finest game of all . . . the noble game of living life first class! There are basic ground rules to living life successfully. We have to find out what they are. And then put them into practice. Knowledge, not applied, gathers dust on the shelf. These rules of life are basic natural laws. Like the law of gravity. Until Isaac Newton came along an apple would still fall from the tree [which meant the law of gravity was present and working and doing very well, thank you] but none of us were aware of the law. No one had bothered to postulate what it meant.

Seeing a jet airliner flash across the sky seems magic to a primitive person living in the jungle. But you and I know it's no miracle—the aircraft is able to defy the law of gravity because of yet another natural law, that of aerodynamics. So it is with the laws of living. They follow a natural law which is as old as the hills. The Law of Karma. Simply, what you give out, you get back. We've been told this by many great teachers: didn't St. Paul say "As a man soweth so shall he reap"? Even today's modern computer terminology has a standard phrase, "garbage in, garbage out." In other words, life is a mirror. It reflects back to us what we project.

Now once we grasp this very simple fact, it can revolutionize our whole way of looking at life. We realize that we are responsible for what happens to us. As the poet W. E. Henley quoth, "I am the Master of my Fate, I am the Captain of my Soul." To reiterate, everything that happens to us, everything that enters our life, good or bad, is the *result* of our own thinking and doing. It's just that simple.

"Wow!" I hear you saying, "What a trip to lay on me. You mean if I'm out of work and hard up, it's not just a lousy blow of fate?"

Exactly. With no one to blame but ourselves. No alibis. No excuses. And when you start to think about it, it makes a lot of sense. Because then everything is explained. Why some people get bad breaks and others get good breaks. Why? After all, there's no sense in God playing favorites. Why would It favor some and not others? It only starts to make sense, to fall into place, when we begin to understand the Law of Karma. It's the original good news/bad news law.

"OK, but how does this Law of Karma work?"

Very simply; everything we think, everything we do causes a reaction.

"Even thoughts?"

Yes. Visualize your thoughts like arrows. Each thought is shot out somewhere, and has to come to rest somewhere, someplace. It can't disappear into limbo. No, each and every thought that passes through our minds, whether weak or strong, sets up a vibration, and that vibration causes an effect.

Now it's true of course that stronger thoughts will result in stronger effects. Especially if they are sustained and repeated for any length of time. Then they build up considerable power.

And the effect of those powerful thoughts is bound to materialize sooner or later in our outer circumstances.

"Why"

Because, scientists tell us, we live in an electromagnetic world. Each of us is surrounded by a field of magnetic energy. And when we project thoughts into that field of magnetic energy, we are influencing it, we are causing the molecules in that field to turn one way or the other, i.e. positively or negatively. When our thoughts are negative then we color the environment around us *negatively,* and we should not be surprised when negative things start to happen to us. Haven't you ever had a day when everything seemed to go wrong? When you bumped into the furniture in a hurry while dressing, your car wouldn't start, and when it did and you hit the freeway the traffic all seemed to cut into you? And walking along the sidewalk everybody seemed to bump into you? And as the morning went on, things got worse and worse. Sure, we all have. What's happening is this—we have turned our mental molecules into a negative direction, and each little negative stimulus is aggravating the situation, and we are charging the mental vibrations around us more and more negatively. So we shouldn't be surprised if things go wrong for us!

But the Law of Attraction—which is really what it is, for we are attracting negative happenings into our experience—works two ways fortunately. We can turn things right around, point them in a positive direction and have them working *for* us—rather than *against* us.

"How do we do that?"

Very simple. Affirm forcibly "I hereby wipe my mind clear of all negative vibrations." Visualize yourself wiping clean a blackboard. "From now on only good, happy, *positive* things can enter my environment." Say this forcibly two or three times to really impress upon your subconscious and let its full import sink in. We are instructing the subconscious part of our mind to react positively to life around us, and we thereby project positive vibrations into our mental atmosphere. No matter what happens we will find ourselves automatically *reacting* positively.

After all, what happens to us is never as important as our *reaction* to what happens. Shakespeare said, "There's naught good nor bad, but thinking makes it so."

This book is not a magic wand. There's no free lunch anywhere. In my publishing days we termed this kind of book a "self-help" book. We sold most of them by direct mail. And we soon discovered an interesting thing: many individuals ordered book after book of the self-help genre. We found that our best prospects for a new help-yourself book were people who previously bought them!

Now if these people, over and over again, kept buying these books, obviously they were not satisfied with what they got in the past. I suspect that if the readers did not get the desired results, they blamed the book; they may not have realized that they needed to do some mental work to achieve their desired results. No, it was the book's fault; therefore if this book didn't work, maybe the next one would. And so they went on buying book after book.

I sincerely hope, dear reader, that you are not like that. Because neither this book, nor any other book, will change your life *unless* you make a determined effort to put into practice the principles outlined herein. You can read all the books on golf you like, all the books you like on bridge, but unless you pluck up courage and get out onto the golf links eventually, or sit down at a bridge foursome, you're never going to be called a player. It's like reading a book on swimming; at some point you've got to dive into the water and start thrashing your arms about as best you can. Same way with life. You can't just read this book. You have to use it. Ideally you should refer to it as an ongoing reference book for practical living. Refer to it every month, say, for five or ten minutes to brush up upon its principles.

But the important point is this: neither this book nor any other book can teach you any magical formulas, any mystical incantations, that will transform your life. It just doesn't work that way.

There's an old Portuguese fishermens' saying: "Pray to God but pull for the shore." In other words, we have to do our part. Understanding the law of gravity is one thing, but we've still got to climb to a height and drop a ball to see it in action.

"God helps those who help themselves," is another true saying.

A word of caution: we shouldn't make the same mistake of believing that if we become "spiritual" then automatically we are gifted with fortune, fame, love, and all the good things of life. We may—or we may not. Or we may get them, but be unable to hold onto them.

Why? Because we are here on earth, in this plane of experience, to learn certain lessons. The University of Life, it's termed by Rev. Domenic A. Polifrone, dynamic minister of the Church of Religious Science.

And that brings us to our next chapter . . .

CHAPTER II

The University of Life

Does life have any meaning to it at all? It certainly must be because otherwise there would be no point to it. When we look up at the sky at night and see the stars and planets in their steady orbits, we realize there has to be a great Intelligence behind all this that is responsible for the orderly course of the universe, and of the millions of other universes, until the mind boggles at it all.

Philosopher John Locke declared that if there were no such being as God we would have to invent Him.

And John Stuart Mill noted that even primitive peoples believe in some form of higher power. Mill went on to postulate that obviously the first action of any superior Being would be to imprint the fact of its existence within the hearts of men.

Whether you believe in God or a Higher Power or not, you have to agree that there is an orderly system in the universe. We have but to look around us and observe that Nature follows an established pattern with the four seasons rotating annually. All of which indicates the high probability that, if there is orderliness to all the other stars and planets and their courses, to the continuing expressions of Nature, that there has to be a similar order and meaning to *our* existences.

"But what?" you say.

Well, it's not too difficult to perceive. Every religion tries to answer that question in its own way. Even scientists have their own theories about systems of evolution, of humankind being the latest expression of the life force. We have but to look around us and observe that the watchword in Nature is change. In all history, nothing stands still; empires rise and fall, yesterday's glories are today's ashes, nothing is permanent. What does this mean to us? Simply that this ongoing tide of energy in human affairs betokens a policy—let's call it evolution.

If we examine closely the whole course of human history we are inexorably forced to the conclusion that there is a meaning to life. There is a clear pattern. For on this tiny planet we are being forced to come together. General Jan Smuts once said that the pattern of the human race is from the family to the tribe to the city-state to the nation and finally to the large power empires. Today we have three blocs in the world—the American, the Russian and the Third World. It is inevitable that within a generation or two we will have a united world. Today we have Europe united economically; that was unthinkable forty years ago.

Yes, there is a spiritual purpose to the universe and a spiritual meaning to our lives. And that meaning is clear: that we are on this plane of experience to learn and grow. You might well term it the University of Life.

"What happens when we graduate," you ask?

Well, then no doubt we go on to another world just as do college graduates. But experience doesn't cease. Meanwhile we have our work cut out for us learning our lessons here.

And that's where our old friend the Law of Karma comes in again. Because basically it arranges for us to repeat experiences *until* we draw the lessons from them. Then we do not have to undergo them again. So, contrary to what many think, Karma is *not* punishment: It is an educative process presenting the circumstances whereby we may learn life's basic lessons.

Inescapably entwined with the Law of Karma is the fact of reincarnation. "How do you know it's a fact," you ask? Because everything points to it. Nature gives us a clear example every year; during winter, it appears a seeming death, everything is cold and the trees are barren, all life has gone. But come spring we witness the miracle of resurrection, of life reasserting itself and Nature is born again. We see the trees and plants blooming and burgeoning into full midsummer strength, and then again comes autumn and the leaves turn brown and wither—and once again everything appears to die.

Another example of reincarnation occurs to us every twenty-four hours when we lie down and our bodies become still and we lose consciousness—yet we come back to them each morning and resume our identities. Is this not a seeming death?

The Egyptians believed that the sun was the symbol of the Creator of the Universe, a spiritual window into the galaxy, and they worshipped it as the source of all life. Yet the sun god Ra died every evening as it sank below the horizon but to reappear each dawn triumphantly in the opposite direction. The Egyptians believed that the sun travelled overnight through the nether world of Hades. Is not this yet again another manifestation of continuing life?

Scientists today tell us that when they split the atom they come down to the minutest particle they can determine and then all is *energy*. And energy cannot be cancelled out. Coal comes from the centuries-old ashes of wood deep in the earth, is burned in our fireplaces and transmuted to warmth and smoke, and then once again the ashes are buried in the earth. The energy of the coal continues in different forms.

We won't go into the innumerable examples of people who claim to remember previous lives. But, merely from the viewpoint of logic, threescore and ten years obviously are insufficient to learn all we need to learn. We need to return here time after time to continue our education. Over the lifetimes we learn our lessons and refine our characters. And that's what it's all about. That's why we're here. And in the next chapter we'll see how we can turn life from mundane existence into a sublime adventure.

CHAPTER III

The Power of Thought

So far we've sketched the philosophy surrounding what life is all about and why we're here. Now we're going to plunge into how to make the best of our existences, how to lead happier, healthier, and more prosperous lives.

Thoughts are things. Yes, every thought passing through our minds is a messenger which we emit into the magnetic field surrounding us. We are always projecting thoughtwise whether we know it or not. We are either projecting *passively* like a straw blown about in the wind, or we are transmitting *actively* when we are controlling our thoughts. Most of the time most of us are merely thinking passively. Like receiving service in a game of tennis. But today's game of tennis, the big game, is won by champions who have terrific control of their serve. They control their game thusly, and in turn we can control our game, the game of life, by controlling our serve, i.e., our active thoughts.

Ralph Waldo Emerson said, "Most people think only once or twice a year. If I think a couple of dozen times a year that makes me a genius." What he meant of course was that most people think *actively* maybe once or twice a year. Well, by learning to think actively part of every day you will see your life transformed and you will begin to attract into it all the good and beautiful things you deserve.

St. Paul said, "Whatever things be noble and beautiful and true, *think on these things.*" What he meant was that we attract to us that which we think about.

Emerson said [you'll note the many quotations in this book from Emerson and St. Paul — simply because they are both very quotable!] "A man is largely what he thinks about all day long." And the Bible says, "As a man thinketh in his heart, so is he." (Proverbs 23:7 King James Version)

Now how does this power of thought work? Let's go back a step. Something created this universe. Most people call it God. And the Bible tells us that man was created in the image of God. Now, if God is the ultimate Creator which created everything around us including ourselves, and we are made in Its image, then surely we ourselves must have some of that power of *creativity* to some extent. And we do. After all, look at the large number of creative artists who have provided us with music, painting, sculpture, poetry, etc. These are certainly all creative people, creators in their own realms.

So can we in our realm, the realm of everyday life, be the masters of the art of living. It's like being the scriptwriter, director and producer of a movie—a movie we star in. So we *can* create our own circumstances by the power of thought. If we don't like our lives we *can* change them.

"Wait a minute," you say. "What about the other people in our lives, you don't mean that we can change them into mere puppets?"

No, that's *not* possible. But we *can* change our relationship with others and our reaction to the part others play in our lives. So to that extent we *are* masters of our fate and can reorient and reconstruct our own lives.

CHAPTER IV

Love Your Enemies—

It Will Drive Them Crazy!

Human relationships present one of the thorniest thickets on life's path. We can't duck the problems they present; that's no solution, they won't go away. But here's a surefire way to handle them.

Life is a boomerang. What we send out is what we get back. So if we harbor thoughts of hate, ill-will, and resentment, it is like hugging a poisonous snake to our bosom. Those feelings will fester and sooner or later will erupt in our physical condition. So, from a practical standpoint, there's nothing to be gained by hating our enemies. We only injure ourselves.

"You don't know the s.o.b. I have to deal with," you say. "If you only knew what he's done to me, blah blah blah, etc."

It doesn't matter who did what to whom. There's only one solution, namely to forgive. No other way works.

This is why Jesus said, "Turn the other cheek." Very practical advice. A lot better than "an eye for an eye, a tooth for a tooth." They had been trying that for thousands of years, and it hadn't worked. Jesus came up with a new way. He said "Love thy neighbor as thyself." Mahatma Gandhi so loved his enemies, the British, that they just couldn't take it and had to quit India. Twenty-five hundred years ago Gautama Buddha pointed out that if we make room in our minds for negative bitter thoughts of complaint or resentment against those who mistreat us, we shall not be free and will remain unable to find peace.

There's nothing more tragic than to observe someone carrying a hatred over the years. It magnifies beyond proportion; and it corrodes the inner lining of a person's soul.

So try the other route. The high road. Think of your enemies, of those who wish you ill, think of them with tolerance and understanding and good will. See them for what they are, and see them without rancor. Think of their good points; everyone has *some* good points. Be objective. Be impartial. What could you like about them? And in your meditations or prayers, send them feelings of good will. Remember Will Rogers' famous dictum: "I never met a man I could not like."

At the same time, if you believe they are emitting feelings of hatred toward *you,* then mentally surround yourself with the sacred white light which protects you and through which no harm can penetrate. Incidentally, if you keep up the practice of sending good will to your enemies, you may find an interesting development: you may well find that your enemies' behavior toward you is changing, becoming friendlier toward you. After all, it takes two to tango!

The power of love is the greatest power in the world. Love is the strongest of all the mental powers. Love is like a pole: at the lower end it is mired in animal lust, toward the middle it reflects personal love of the Hollywood type (which beguiles too many youngsters into early marriages eventuating in divorce), and higher on the pole it reflects one-on-one love, a finer kind of love approximating the soulmate principle. Then farther up the pole we find what the Greeks called *agape* which means a tolerance and a goodwill to all. And finally, at the top of the pole, we find the sage-like quality of compassion for all mankind, the compassion which causes an adept to reincarnate again and again in the service of humanity. This is the grand goal to which we can all aspire. And if it seems an impossible dream, let us remember that the goal *has* been achieved, therefore it *is* possible. If during the trials and tribulations of our quest on earth, the way seems long and hard, we can console ourselves with the knowledge that this too is a two way street, that just as we are seeking the Higher Power, so It is receptive to us and attracting us to It as a magnet attracts iron.

If our desire to achieve the goal is overwhelming and if our faith be there, then sooner or later we shall realize the grand purpose of our life here on earth.

As Emerson put it so beautifully, "Man's welfare is dear to the heart of Being."

CHAPTER V

What's Your Problem?

Plato said that inherent in every problem is a solution. He went on to say it's like a two-sided coin—you can't have one without the other.

But why do we have problems at all? Why does God allow them? Ah ha, that's the whole point. Without problems, life would have little meaning; we would merely be eking out a bovine existence.

My lovely Chinese daughter, Suk Fun, tells me that the Chinese word for problem is the same as that for opportunity.

Once we realize we are all students in the University of Life, everything falls into place. Problems are challenges whereby we grow. Without them, how would we master our lessons? Just as steel has to be tempered in fire else it would easily break, so we need to be tempered in the crucible of life's experiences.

Looking at it this way we see that problems are indeed *opportunities;* how we react to them and cope with them determines how quickly we progress through life's school.

"That's all very well," you say, "but my problems are usually pretty difficult, and sometimes downright painful." Granted, my friend, but if they weren't, would they really have much meaning? It's only when problems make an impact on us that we pay much notice to them; they are signals claiming our attention.

And here's a comforting thought. God never sends us a problem we are incapable of handling. Why would It? That wouldn't make sense. Problems are not intended as punishment but as opportunities for learning. So we never receive more than we can deal with. Every problem has a built-in solution.

How do we find that solution? Well, in addition to using all the normal approaches, our intellect, our mind's reasoning power, etc., we should never neglect to call upon help from the Higher Power through prayer and meditation. That can overcome *all* obstacles. "With God all things are possible."

Of course, it's not just the major afflictions which come into our lives. There are also those common everyday bogies which plague people—like anger, guilt, impatience, fear. Some specific tips to help you combat and overcome these nuisances follow:

Anger? Breathe slowly and deeply, i.e., the very opposite of someone who is agitated. At the same time ask yourself, "Who is angry?" Try to step aside and become an observer rather than a participant. This technique is guaranteed to dissipate your anger. Try it!

Guilt? It's so easy to slip into self-recrimination. We all do it. But there's a quick surefire cure. Stop brooding, let go of the old. Think *now*. As St. Paul put it, "Forgetting those things which are behind, I press on toward the mark."

Impatient? Then apply the brakes. Cool it! Literally force yourself to slow down—think slower, move slower. If you speed up to sneak through a traffic light that's turning red, then penalize yourself by driving around the block and come back again. You'll learn!

Afraid? Perhaps the most prevalent goblin of all. Fortunately fear can be banished by a simple technique. Ralph Waldo Emerson gave it to us: "Do the thing you fear, and the death of fear is certain." Yes, action is the key to casting out fear. Fear festers best at three a.m. when we lie helpless in our beds. Comes the dawn, however, and we can be too busy to entertain this unwelcome guest.

Next time you face a problem, switch your thinking onto a *positive* set of tracks. Know that the solution exists. Don't hesitate to pray for help from the Higher Power. "Ask and ye shall receive." So choose the high road. Set the positive wheels in motion. Resolve to show forth your Better Self. This way you enlist the aid of powerful forces. "If God be for us, who can be against us?"

"God's in his heaven and all's right with the world" wrote the poet Robert Browning. Yes, if we could but see behind appearances, we would *know* that God is indeed running the show like a gigantic spiritual computer. And that everything that happens to us, happens for the best—if we *make* it happen for the best!

CHAPTER VI

Life is a Mirror

What you see is what you get. It has to be. Because life reflects back to you what *you* are and how you think. So, look around you. Do you like what you see? You created your circumstances. No one else is responsible. You may find this hard to swallow, but it's true. We make our own world. No alibis, no excuses.

The Hindus call this the Law of Karma, of cause and effect. St. Paul decreed, "As a man soweth, so shall he reap."

Life is like a computer. We are constantly programming it—for better or worse. What we feed into it eventually comes back to us.

The good news is that if we do not like our present circumstances we can do something about it! Because God has granted us the priceless boon of *choice*. We can choose the type of person we want to be, the kind of life we want to enjoy.

We always have a choice. If you go into a florist's and order a dozen roses, and when he brings the roses you don't like the look of them, you can always change your mind and say, "Oh, I think I'd rather have tulips instead." No problem. He may give you a dirty look but he'll go and fetch the tulips. You can order what you want.

Same with life. You can choose what you want—as long as it's moral and ethical. So why not choose the *best?* Set your sights high. There's a current saying, "Today is the first day of the rest of my life." Each dawn is a fresh beginning. Each day is a brand new deal.

Emerson said, "Enthusiasm is the powerful engine of success." So why not greet the morn with enthusiasm?

"But what if I don't feel enthusiastic?" you ask.

There's a simple solution: *pretend* to be enthusiastic, act enthusiastic, and very quickly you'll feel that ol' enthusiasm tingling through your veins and brightening your outlook. The word enthusiasm stems from the Greek words "En-theos" which means "to be in God." Isn't that great?

What's more, you'll attract good things into your day because you are now transmitting *positive* vibrations. And remember what you give out is what you get back. There's no way around the rule. So why not turn it to your advantage. Put your best *look* forward—life will reflect it from all sides!

CHAPTER VII

The Law of Attraction

This is a very simple law. Like the law of gravity. And it works just as effectively. Simply put, you get what you think about. This is such an obvious law that it's a wonder everyone doesn't realize it.

At school they taught us that opposite attracts. But in real life, it's different. Like attracts like. You attract to you what you are, what you think.

The Law of Attraction is really the key to all the other laws. For instance, the Law of Karma, which is the law of cause and effect, of reaping what we have sowed, is the *result* of your thinking and doing. But the Law of Attraction is what caused you to do those actions in the first place!

"How does the Law of Attraction work?"

It's quite simple. We exist in an electro-magnetic field. When we think positively, we charge the field around us with positive vibrations. And when we think negatively, we charge it with negative vibrations.

It's hard to have our minds in "neutral." Most of the time we are projecting positively or negatively.

It bears repeating, when we project positively, we attract *positive* circumstances to us. And the reverse when we transmit negatively.

You can put the power of attraction to work for you at any time to influence events in your favor.

The best way I can illustrate this for you is to give you some personal examples from my own experience:

One Sunday night I was driving home from New York City about 10:00 p.m. and as I came up the approach to the George Washington bridge I hit a deep pothole. Bang! I heard one of my hubcaps fly off. I stopped the car and went looking for my hubcap. [This is not exactly a safe thing to do on the West Side highway, but I didn't stop to think.] I didn't find *my* hubcap, but found two others just like it! Crossing the George Washington bridge I became aware of an ominous sound, "Thunk! Thunk! Thunk!" I wasn't sure what was wrong but realized I had better check it out as soon as possible. And I knew that I had better do some mental work to ensure that my car, Constanza, and I emerged safely from this situation. So I affirmed strongly to myself, "Despite any appearances to the contrary, Constanza and I are fully protected, and perfectly safe, and whatever needs correcting will be corrected and we will be able to get home to sleep in our own bed [and garage] tonight!"

And I held to that thought strongly. As we came off the bridge onto Route 9W I looked in vain for an open gas station. Down the road I finally saw the lights of an open station. Gratefully I pulled in, got out of the car, and saw that my rear left tire was completely flat. I asked the attendant if he would change it for me.

"I'm just closing," he said.

"But I would be very grateful if you wouldn't mind doing me this favor."

"No, you don't understand," he said, "if people see my lights on they will come in for gas and I'll never finish your tire or be able to get home tonight."

"But I want to get home too," I said, and I kept talking. Suddenly, "I'll do it for you," he said.

He changed the tire quickly, and did a good job, whereupon I thanked him and gave him ten dollars.

He was a modest young man. "But this is much too much," he said.

"But I want to show my appreciation and thank you for helping me out, and I want to encourage you to help other people in distress."

So Constanza and I did get home safely that night, and next day I went back to pick up the punctured tire which had been repaired and I told the station owner about the good deed his young mechanic had done for me. I hope it did him some good.

But the point I want to make is that as soon as I knew something was wrong I immediately put my positive thinking into high gear and affirmed that everything would work out alright. I did this quietly and calmly but full of conviction.

You see, we can't prevent unpleasant events coming into our lives, like flat tires, but we *can* control our reaction to them, and by positively charging the vibrations around us we can ameliorate their effect—we can land on our feet every time. The trick is to start the positive vibrations humming *immediately*. Don't give way to any negative impulses.

Incidentally, it's been years since I was ever stuck on a highway with a flat tire. Usually I find them in my garage in the morning when it's a simple matter to phone the station down the hill to come up and fix it. You see, I don't *expect* to be let down on the highway by any sort of problem. Remember two things: use the technique of enveloping your car with white light in a safety bubble to prevent any harm coming to you or the car; do this mentally as soon as you step into your auto. And use the affirmation that you and the car will reach your destination safe and sound.

Why *white* light? Because this is the closest we can come to visualizing the Higher Power. Think of it as God-stuff, if you like. It has no physical shape, no form, no coloring. It's *pure.* St. John's gospel opens with a reference to the light shining in the darkness. St. Paul encountered "a light from heaven" on the road to Damascus. Many mystics and near-death experiences tell of a celestial being of light. So we associate light as the physical essence of God. And we can harness this white light to mentally protect ourselves and our possessions. We can visualize it enfolding loved ones who are ill.

A concentrated strong affirmation or positive prayer can produce almost *instantaneous* results. But equally potent can be a frame of mind or an attitude or slight wish if maintained over a sufficient period of time. For instance, I was born and raised in England where Tudor style architecture is quite prevalent. I said to myself one day I would like to have a home in Tudor-style. In fact, I'm not sure I really even said it to myself, but I do know that I had a liking for Tudor architecture. After the Second World War, I came to live in America. Well, you'll admit, there are not too many Tudor style homes in the USA. So you wouldn't place any big bets on my ending up in one. But that's what happened! Even to imitation lattice windows!

The moral is "Be careful what you want, because you may get it!"

Being a busy executive, I often write notes to myself on pieces of paper and shove them in my pockets. At home,

I sort them out on my bureau for follow up next morning. I found myself in the habit of reminding myself to get gasoline by simply writing "Get gas!" Well, I got gas alright. I started getting these pains in my chest! So I phoned my favorite spiritual practitioner, Alma Tesch, and told her my problem. She said "Well you know we're not allowed to diagnose but I had chest pains like that recently and it turned out to be gas." She suggested we do a positive prayer together. Alma affirmed "You are in perfect health. Your body vibrates radiantly with exuberant health. Every organ and muscle and cell of your body is in harmony and working together for good." As Alma spoke, I felt a tingling go through my body. Just like an electrical charge. I mentioned this to her and she said she also felt it! So even though we were separated by some twenty miles, nevertheless we both felt this healing surge of power. And why not? After all the Infinite can be everywhere, and is everywhere, and we were tuned into each other on a mental wavelength. My gas pains disappeared instantly and even though I had planned to visit a doctor the next morning for diagnosis, there was no need to do so. Oh yes, I still write notes to myself, but now I write "get fuel!"

An artist friend has a studio in a run down area. Some of her neighbors are drug takers and often hold noisy parties with unsavory friends. So my friend made a series of scientific prayers (another name for concentrated mental affirmations) and requested protection. Well, she received her protection alright. One morning she went out to find a large German Shepherd lying on her doorstep, weak and sick and altogether in bad shape. My friend Erna is a kindly soul so she took the dog in and nursed it and fed it. And fed it. And fed it. And fed it and fed it because that dog could sure eat! She found it was costing her a fortune to feed the dog, much more than she could afford, but the dog gave her protection alright. If anyone came near Erna's door the dog would bark loudly and ferociously. But Erna just could not afford to keep her and had to arrange to give her away.

"Next time, Erna" I said. "Pray for a small dog with a big bark!" It pays to be specific, to ask for *exactly* what we want.

Consider the case of the monk stranded in the desert miles from anywhere who prayed for a horse. Lo and behold, on the horizon he saw a small cloud of dust which turned out to be a party of brigands who stopped near the monk to rest their horses in the shade of a tree. Suddenly, one of the brigand's horses gave birth to a foal. The brigand chief looked around, saw the monk and ordered, "Here you, carry my foal!" So the monk got his wish—he got his horse—but he omitted to state who should be carrying who!

Another example: each January I make my New Year's resolutions, just like you and everyone else. A good idea, incidentally, because there's a lot of value in this old tradition. We wipe the slate clean, let go of the old year, and start a brand new existence and we postulate the better person we intend to be by means of these resolutions.

I include in my annual resolutions the perennial one to lose weight. [Actually one shouldn't say, *lose* weight because that implies we could find it again! Better to declare to *shed* or give away weight.] So last January 1st I tacked up a sign on my bathroom mirror, "I weigh 168 pounds!" Guess what? Within a few days I came down with the flu and spent five days in bed, and was unable to eat solid food—in fact I always fast when I become ill just like animals do—and very quickly shed poundage, yes, you guessed it, at the end of my enforced fast I weighed exactly 168 pounds! But that was making it the hard way. So next year my resolution will read, "I weigh 168 pounds in a *healthy* body!"

I could give you lots of such examples. The fact is that the power of our mind, what we call the subconscious [wrongly, it's more like the *super-conscious*] gives us what we specify and grants our wishes like a magic genie. This is because we are consciously or unconsciously using this force all the time, just as sunlight is everywhere around us and if we take a magnifying glass we can harness that sun's rays and concentrate them powerfully so they will set fire to a piece of paper. Diffused dreamy imagining usually will not do the trick. Our thought patterns must be focused sharply.

This power and its use has been identified by many names. Perhaps the best known is *positive thinking.* The world owes a debt to Norman Vincent Peale who made this phrase so well-known with his best selling book "The Power of Positive Thinking." Dr. Peale yoked the power of this force to his own strong belief in Christianity. But it will work for followers of any religion or even for those of none at all. In fact, like yoga, it is not a religion, it is a technique, a mental technique, using a scientific law of Mind.

This power works just as well—just as effectively—on a national or international level, as it does in everyday events of our personal lives. I remember being in England when Winston Churchill became Prime Minister in June 1940. The country had just suffered the traumatic anguish of Dunkirk. We were expecting to be invaded momentarily. The national mood was one of gloom and impending doom. Negativism hung like a pall over the country. Then Churchill took the reins. He made his famous speech, "We will fight on the beaches, we will fight in the hills, we will fight in the streets—we will *never* surrender!" Overnight a wave of *positive* thinking swept the country. The nation was galvanized into an upbeat attitude. Maybe we had our backs to the wall, but we knew where we stood, and we wouldn't retreat one more inch! Thus, as the 17th century poet,

Alexander Pope said, "The pen is mightier than the sword," and in this case Churchill's magnificent oratory was worth a hundred divisions. He transformed England and led it onward to ultimate victory.

Another magnificent example of national transformation through the positive mental attitude of its leader is of course closer to home, right here in the United States. Remember how the jaunty smile of Franklin Delano Roosevelt exuded confidence? It not only swept him into the White House in 1932 but was a potent weapon in the arsenal against the big depression of that time. FDR declared, "The only thing we have to fear is *fear* itself." How right he was. And he proved it by leading this country out of the depression.

Yet another example of a national leader who attained his ends through the power of mind is Mahatma Gandhi. He instigated a *non-violent* revolution, the first in history. Where the sword and bloodshed had failed, Gandhi succeeded in enjoining his countrymen through the power of something far superior. His determined mental attitude enabled him to overcome insuperable obstacles.

So there you have it. The Law of Attraction. How it works. The Law of Attraction is the key to a successful, happier and more prosperous life. Let it transform *your* existence . . . *today!*

CHAPTER VIII

Watch Your Consciousness!

Who are the victims of muggings and other street crimes so prevalent in our society today? I'll tell you. The people who avidly devour news of such crimes in the newspapers and on television. They are setting themselves up as victims because they are filling their minds with these events. And what we give our attention to . . . is bound to come into our lives. In other words, whatever we fill our minds with, is bound to materialize in our lives sooner or later.

That's why the worst thing we can do is watch the ten o'clock news just before we go to bed. Because we're stuffing our consciousness with all the [usually bad] news of the day. I'd rather go to sleep with a cobra under my pillow!

Same thing in the morning. It's all right to have a clock radio alarm to wake us up so long as we have it tuned to a music station. To be blasted into wakefulness by an announcer's rasping voice giving us all the negative things which have occurred around the world during the night is no way to start the day!

Ideally we should wake up gently to bring back with us the vibrations of the other world in which we have been immersed for several hours. We should lie still and try to recall our dreams, and then write them down, to ponder over and decipher later.

And we would do far better to fill our minds with a few positive affirmations to help us start the day in the right mood rather than listen passively to an onslaught of news garbage.

No news is good news

"But I have to keep up with what's going on in the world," you object.

Why? Most happenings in the world don't concern us anyway, especially the negative and gruesome and horrible happenings so prevalent. Certainly we do need to know about the important national and international affairs, but we can garner these from the five minute newscasts given on the hour by many radio stations.

The point is, we need to be very careful what we allow into our consciousness. Because, as said earlier, if maintained over a period of time it will definitely emerge into our lives.

From now on, when you see anything unpleasant, ask yourself, "Do I want this in my life?" If not, then switch your attention immediately, otherwise you may get what your attention is focused on.

CHAPTER IX

Visualize Your Way to Success

I'm talking into my pocket recorder while driving back from Scranton, PA. In fact nearly all this book has been dictated, in my car while I'm traveling. So if the text sounds somewhat informal to you, that's the reason. In any case, I like to think I'm talking just to *you* as we drive along, having a friendly conversation.

A few years ago someone asked me, "What do you plan to do when you retire?"

I replied, "Well, I'd like to concentrate on the spiritual side of life, studying, writing, lecturing, passing on information I've learned that may help others." Incidentally, I consider it a basic spiritual rule to pass on what we have learned. Otherwise it's like being handed a candle in a dark room—and blowing it out!

"And, while I wouldn't want it full time, I've always hankered to lecture at a college. I would like that. But there's not much chance as I've had no teaching experience and I certainly have no qualifications in that field."

Yet, here I am . . . driving home to New York after having just given a lecture on publishing at the University of Scranton. I'm feeling good about it. I liked being on the campus, mixing with young students, and I felt very much at ease talking to them in the classroom. So I have achieved my wish—despite lack of experience or qualifications!

In fact, many of the spiritual-type organizational activities at which I lecture and give workshops these days are on campuses of attractive colleges such as Rosemont College outside Philadelphia, Lake Forest in Illinois, or Elizabethtown in Pennsylvania. I enjoy the campus atmosphere. So that which I desired, hath come to pass!

What does this show? Simply that we attract into our lives that which we desire. And all hurdles can be overcome; in my case, lack of experience and qualifications. But this did not prevent Life from granting my desire and bringing it about. I now find myself with at least half a dozen such teaching assignments a year. Which is just about right.

What Billie Jean King taught me

No, it wasn't about tennis. Unfortunately. My game could use it. But some years ago I read an interview with Billie Jean King, then the reigning champion of women's tennis. She said that before every important game she would spend the evening sitting in an armchair and visualizing the match, imagining each serve or return of her opponent and *then* imaging her own *reaction* to her opponent's ball. She knew her opponents, of course, and had seen them play on television several times and would watch a video tape of a recent game to observe her opponent's style, technique and strategies.

So that when Billie Jean got on the court next day her mind was pre-programmed to cope with any situation. And regardless of what her opponent did with the ball, Billie Jean would know how to handle that shot, in fact, she *automatically* reached for the best shot to handle the situation *because* she was ingrained mentally with a groove into which she fell without even having to think in the split-second timing required of her.

And later that day Billie Jean said she would watch a video tape of the game and see where she could have played better. You might say she was mentally *replaying* those situations which called for better strategy or control of the ball. Thus she was again programming her mind to deal automatically with such situations when they occurred in a future game.

So if Billie Jean's technique works on the tennis court why shouldn't it work in a much more important game, the game of life itself!

More recently I read in *U.S. News & World Report* that before he takes a swing, golf champ Jack Nicklaus imagines the ball in flight, sailing down the fairway and landing where he wants it to land. He attributes 50 percent of his success to this mental preparation.

Many top business leaders do the same type of mental rehearsal to prepare for pressure situations. One corporate president reviews a victory log of past successes before a tough presentation to increase his confidence. Many executives imagine themselves as Nicklaus does, successfully meeting challenges of the morrow.

The night before teaching or lecturing, I make it a point to *visualize* myself standing up before the group and enunciating clearly, speaking distinctly and with confidence and authority and projecting an air of sincerity and warmth. And I refresh and strengthen this image next day while going to my assignment. The result is that's exactly what happens. So while I've studied the technical aspects of public speaking, and taken courses in it, I embellish these through the power of mind and harnessing my subconscious [I think it should be called *super-conscious*] to work for me in projecting a favorable image. And so I find myself much in demand as a speaker.

You can too. People often say to me, "Gee, I wish I had your gifts for public speaking. You seem so natural up there." Well, as I've said, you have to learn the technical part of whatever vocation or sport you desire to shine in, but this is not enough. You can play the piano with technical accuracy, for instance, but to be a professional pianist you must figuratively reach out and involve your audience. That's where the power of visualization comes in.

You can be *surer* of creating a favorable impression by programming yourself mentally beforehand. Latch onto the power of your subconscious to aid you. Let it carve a mental groove into which you can fall easily when the time comes to help you put your best foot forward. Just visualize yourself acting or performing the way you'd like, and lo and behold it will come about!

How to put visualization to work for you

Best time is at night, before going to sleep, so your subconscious can take over and do the work for you while you are asleep. By morning a definite pattern will be etched in your mind. See yourself in the situation which will occur the next day. Let's say you are a sales person or going to an important meeting: visualize yourself objectively acting and *reacting* the way you would like to. A word of caution: *do not* try to visualize the other person's response. This is manipulation, and borders on black magic. It is morally wrong and can bring bad consequences. So avoid that. Just do *your* part, and don't worry about the results. This is the advice that Krishna gave to Arjuna in the Bhagavad Gita, when the Lord was counseling the young prince on how to go into battle. "Do your duty but be unconcerned about results."

I cannot overemphasize the importance of visualization. It can be the key to your creating a happier, healthier and more successful life for yourself. Try it, you'll be glad you did!

CHAPTER X

Bless 'Em All

During World War II there was a very popular song in the Royal Air Force:

> "Bless 'em all,
> The long and the short and the tall,
> Bless all the sergeants and w.o. ones,
> Bless all the corporals
>   and their blinking sons!"

Applied to today's living, this is a good habit to get into. Blessing everything we encounter, everything around us. For instance, why not bless your car when you get into it. And when you shut it off in the garage. Bless your washing machine when you press the button to spin it into action. Bless the refrigerator in your kitchen. Bless your hot water tank. Bless all these mechanical devices which form so large a part of your life and in blessing them, you are thanking them for doing their job and encouraging them to keep doing it and doing it well.

You see, all these things have a degree of consciousness. Admittedly it's a low degree, but nevertheless it's there and to some extent they can determine our attitude toward them. Ill-natured people who continually curse the appliances in their homes are sure to have those appliances breaking down and giving trouble. I can tell you I seldom have trouble with the appliances in my home simply because I bless them before and after their operations. I thank them for doing their duty, their "dharma," as the Buddhists would say, for this they were born.

I have always had a personal relationship with automobiles. I name them, and for some reason I always choose Italian names. And they are always feminine, just like sailors refer to their ships as feminine. [And that's something else; any sailor will tell you that a ship has "vibes." Immediately upon boarding a sailor can tell whether she's a happy ship or not.]

My present car is Constanza. And every morning upon opening the garage door I say, "Good morning, Constanza!" to her. As I start the engine and ease her out of the garage, I visualize both of us surrounded by a large white bubble, a bubble of protection into which no harm can come. And as we drive along the highway, I thank Constanza for doing her thing and affirm that she will get us to our destination safely and securely and that all the parts of her being, from engine to transmission to wheels, are working perfectly and in good order.

Of all kinds of mechanical equipment, I think automobiles have the highest degree of consciousness. At some point the car and its driver become one. You can tell a lot about a person by examining their car, just as you can tell by examining their household pets. People who mistreat their cars cannot complain if the cars do not come to their rescue in tight corners. For instance, one morning I drove out of my garage onto a sheet of ice and found myself slipping helplessly down to a row of parked cars. "Oh, please Regina [that was the name of my previous car] please help us. I've always loved you, I've always taken good care of you, I've taken you to the beauty shop [car wash] every week, *please* help!" And Regina did. She stopped with her nose literally only one inch from hitting another car. You might say it's just a coincidence or I'm imagining it. Well, you're welcome to your opinion but I believe in mine. There have been too many similar instances where my cars have really helped me out and avoided damage to themselves and others. They know that I take good care of them, and that I love them, take pride in their appearance and well-being. *And they respond.*

Each car I've owned has had its own personality, even the ones I've rented, poor things, as they usually feel prostituted by having so many different drivers. I never allow my car to be taken at a valet parking lot. I'll tip the car hop, but insist on parking myself. My cars have been as different as people, and I treat them differently and talk to them according to their individual personalities. But I love them all and I show that love. People may laugh, that's alright, I don't care!

Notice how your friends treat [or mistreat] their animals? People who are always shouting at their animals thereby display their own insecurity complexes and their need to take it out on a poor helpless creature. But the Law of Karma is invincible and they will be repaid in kind one day. We are literally the guardians of the animal world, and it is our sacred duty to look after them and protect them and train them for their eventual development into the human existence.

A final word about cars. They love to do that for which they were born, to be out on the highway. They don't like being cooped up in the garage. When I open the garage door and release Constanza, her engine fires readily and she is friskily impatient, raring to go. She just can't wait to get down on the roadway and get moving. Especially on a beautiful sunny day. Can't say I blame her, that's when I enjoy it most too!

Many of you say grace before meals. This is a time-honored and hallowed tradition. It has a practical purpose. It provides a pause for us to slow down and detach ourselves from the bustle of preparing the meal or other activities. And it alerts the forces of our body to receive nourishment and be ready to assimilate it. Cup your hands around your plate and affirm that the food is cleansed of any negative influences from any handling during its journey to your table—perhaps the trucker or supermarket clerk was in a bad mood—and now you are purifying it. This is the same principle as that of "prasad"—holy food from the altar.

But how many of you say grace *after* a meal? Why not? It serves an equally practical purpose: to bless the food which we've taken and to facilitate its absorption into ourselves and transmutation into living energy.

In fact, it's not a bad idea to get into the habit of bestowing blessings throughout the day. Bless your car when you're driving in it. Bless the cars around you. Bless the people you come into contact with [inwardly of course]. Bless your surroundings and circumstances. You'll be pleasantly surprised how this practice can soothe your environment and create harmonious circumstances around you.

CHAPTER XI

Self Healing Techniques

There are numerous self healing techniques of many kinds. One of the most effective is visualization. In an earlier chapter we described how to use visualization to program yourself for the events of the coming day, for success in business, etc. Visualization can also be used for healing—both yourself and others.

First, a word of caution. No one seems to really know much about healing or how it works. During the past few years I have read numerous books on healing and have traveled around the country interviewing healers. One of the most famous of them, the late Olga Worrall, told me over lunch in Baltimore, that although she had been the instrument for producing many miraculous cures over the years, she herself still did not know how it worked. "I'm just a housewife," she said, "I even do windows. All I know is sometimes it works, sometimes it doesn't." Yet Mrs. Worrall was the most celebrated healer I've met. She had countless cures on record. Once, to discount the role patients' feelings and emotions might play in the healing process, she went on TV showing she could heal bacteria just by putting her hands around a container of them.

All healers agree that sometimes it works and sometimes it doesn't. They also agree that they themselves do not do the healing; they are merely the instruments through which the healing force comes. A couple of years ago I was invited by a Methodist minister to participate in a laying-on-hands healing service. "Come now," I said, "I know nothing about healing." But my minister friend persisted. So I found myself in front of the altar with the other minister healers. People came forward and I found a man standing in front of me. I put my hands on his shoulders lightly and closed my eyes and visualized the ball of white light that I usually see in meditation. I envisioned beams streaming down from this light encircling both the healee and myself. As I did so I became conscious of a force like an electrical charge and I felt myself becoming very warm. Soon the perspiration was dripping off me. I whispered in the man's ear, "Your body vibrates with radiant health!" As he left the chancel I sent a non-possessive compassionate love toward him and shifted my mental gears into neutral to await the next person to approach me. A month later that man telephoned me to say that he was completely cured of an illness which had plagued him for many years. I was glad, of course, but I had no idea how it happened—and still don't to this day.

I have a theory, for what it's worth. Namely, that sickness can only exist in the lower vibrations of this material world. On a more spiritual plane with finer vibrations, sickness would be unthinkable and therefore cannot exist there. So that if the healee's consciousness is raised to a higher plane of finer vibrations, the sickness just disappears! Perhaps that's what happened in this case.

Anyway, in this chapter I want to share with you a few tips which I have found useful in self healing work. They have worked for me and for others. They may for you too.

> 1) If you have an ache or pain, or a sore muscle, visualize the hand of God gently massaging a white healing ointment into the affected parts. Softly and soothingly the hand's healing power penetrates and brings balm to the distressed part of your body.

> 2) If you have a minor cut, apply Vitamin E ointment and a bandaid and then visualize the white cells of your body running to the rescue and forming a ring around the cut to prevent infection. You can sometimes see this white ring around the cut. These are your body's defenses coming to the rescue. Imagine them as life intelligences, a first aid squad employed by the body for just such emergencies. Kiss your wound and mentally affirm "You are healing, healing, healing!"

> 3) The body has its own inherent healing power. This force will flow through and perform remarkable healings if it is not obstructed. We have to practice the basic rules of hygiene—get enough rest, exercise, eat the proper nutritious live fresh foods (particularly plenty of raw salads), avoid abusing the body with alcohol or tobacco or drugs, give the organs a rest once in a while with short fasts of 36 to 48 hours, have a colonic irrigation cleansing once or twice a year—all this allows the body to let its own healing energy flow unimpeded.

4) These healing energies will operate all the more effectively if we maintain an upbeat, cheerful attitude toward life. "A merry heart is the best medicine," says the Bible. A sunny disposition allows for no clouds wherein illness can fester.

5) During your sunrise or sunset meditations, direct the sun's rays to the dis-eased part of your body. Envision their healing force repairing worn tissue, rebuilding, renewing. This is similar to radiation therapy techniques used in modern medicine.

Prosperity is a state of mind. So is good health. For example, while traveling recently in India I developed sharp pains in my shoulder and right down my arm. I went to a local doctor and then to an osteosurgeon at a major hospital who diagnosed my case as *spondilitis.* Ihad never heard of it. In fact it sounded to me like the spinach pie they serve in Greek diners! But next thing I knew my arm was in a splint and I was going twice a day for traction at the hospital. I also found I could not sleep lying down because the pain in my arm would be irritated in any position. I could only gain relief by sleeping upright in an armchair. So there I was, staying at a five star hotel and I might as well have been sleeping in a chair in the lobby! I also wondered what the maids thought in the morning, finding the bed unused; either I was a playboy out on the town every night or maybe I was a vampire!

When I returned to the States my own doctor informed me that it was osteoarthritis, a degeneration of the vertebrae which causes them to press down upon the nerve extending down the arm. Nothing can be done about it, he said, it's a common practice with aging. Well, I refused to accept this verdict and returned to the holistic health center[2] I attend for chelation under the well-known Dr. Michael B. Schacter. He prescribed a course of herbal medication and minerals and treatments of electrical charge on the machine known as an acuscope. This, combined with expert manipulative adjustments from my chiropracter, Dr. Jack Boshes of New City, NY, certainly afforded much relief. But I could not rid myself completely of the tingling down my arm and the stiffness in two fingers, making it difficult to write.

It was not until I attended a conference of the Spiritual Advisory Council[3] in Chicago a few weeks later that I was completely cured. SAC President, Rev. Paul V. Johnson, introduced me to a psychic healer, Carole Young, who told me to visualize bits of debris cluttering up my vertebrae thereby causing the pressure on the nerve—and to image a vacuum cleaner with powerful suction drawing out all that debris. The treatment worked! I still visualize the vacuum cleaner technique as a preventative and I've had no recurrence of the pain.

Of course, it's not enough merely to obtain a physical healing. It's necessary to find out the *cause* of the sickness and eradicate that too—otherwise the illness will manifest again. Most illnesses stem from a mental/emotional factor; this has to be diagnosed and worked on. Otherwise the illness is likely to recur. It's like cutting down a weed; the only way to stop it from growing again is to dig down into the earth and pull out the roots.

There's an old saying, "As within, so without." If we allow faulty thinking to fester negative emotions in our

---

[2]Mountainview Medical Associates, P.C., Nyack, NY 10960

[3]Spiritual Advisory Council, 2965 W. State Road 434, Suite 300, Longwood, FL 32779

makeup, then they are bound to manifest externally at some point.

An essential ingredient in any healing is a positive, happy, firm expectation that the healing will take place. In fact, such an attitude of "great expectations" is a good way to face the world every day!

Why?

Because our body cells do have consciousness. They are affected by our emotions. When we are cheerful (and especially if we think of them at that time) they *respond* . . . and become charged with positiveness. This enables them to combat and overcome onslaughts by dis-ease to the body. Likewise, if we think and feel dispirited, this encourages disease and the cells are too worn down to act strongly against it. So we are free to choose our Good—or to block it. Make friends with the cells in your body. Talk to them. Send them loving thoughts. Thank them and bless them for being healthy expressions of life. They'll respond in kind!

CHAPTER XII

What's Blocking
Your Prosperity?

Abundance is a natural state. After all, why would God want us to be poor? That would be limiting Its Infiniteness. And that just doesn't make sense. Besides, God creates abundance all around us. Just look at the myriad array of flora and fauna afforded by Nature. God doesn't provide just *one* kind of flower. No! It supplies *hundreds* of different flowers, different plants, different trees. That's abundance! And our planet provides all the food we need; only poor management and corruption prevent its proper distribution. Indeed, God rains abundance upon us. So if we are not prosperous, then obviously the fault is ours—we don't have our bucket out to catch our share. *We* are creating the blockage. Don't let us blame God! "The fault, dear Brutus, lies not in our stars, but in our selves."

But first let us be sure what prosperity is. Ask a dozen people and chances are they will reply, "Money." Nothing could be further from the truth! Money is merely pieces of paper. If you were suddenly stranded in a jungle, what good would a briefcase jammed with money do you? Prosperity then would be represented by food and clothing and shelter, certainly not by pieces of paper.

Remember Mark Twain's classic story, "The Million Pound Note"? How the merchants of London were at the feet of the supposedly wealthy American who brandished a million pound note for which none of them had change? Until he mislaid it . . . and then they were all at his throat demanding payment! The moral here is that it's not money itself we need, but the *things* money will buy us. Let us be clear in our thinking then that money is merely a means to an end, *not* the end itself.

So what we really want is . . . *abundance.* That is our keyword. And it can best be defined as: "The freedom to do *what* we want *when* we want *plus* the wherewithal to do it."

Do not make the mistake of praying for a million dollars, for instance. Instead ask for financial freedom. But do not try to dictate the channels through which it flows. The Higher Power knows best *how* to supply your financial good. Just affirm daily "All my needs are always met."

The art of prosperity thinking is not difficult. But like any other skill one must master its rules and apply them. It's no different from learning to be a good bridge player or golfer.

Here are five guidelines for developing a prosperity consciousness:

> 1) First and foremost . . . TITHE. Give regularly to the source whence you derive your good. It's vital to open a free-flowing stream for abundance to pour in. "Nature abhors a vacuum." So make room for your new good to

come in. Check your closet and give away any clothes you haven't worn recently.

2) Then . . . be sure to give to *yourself.* Pay yourself *before* you pay the butcher, the baker and the candlestickmaker. Put at least 10% of your income into savings; then you're free to spend the balance. If your employer called you in and told you he had to cut your salary by 10%, you could manage. You might not like it, but you *could* manage. So that ten percent is yours, all yours, and the magic of compound interest will go to work for you to make it grow and grow and grow.

3) Buy "twosomes" at the store (especially when they are on sale). Keep a well stocked larder. Your pantry should reflect prosperity. Create an air of opulence in your kitchen. Have several cans of coffee, soup, beans or whatever on your shelves. (A side benefit is you'll never run out.)

4) Treat money with respect. Don't squander it. Spend it . . . but spend it wisely. Straighten the creases out of bills as you tuck them neatly into your billfold—and bless them inwardly. Money will go where it's loved. So don't mistreat it, don't crumple bills.

5) Poverty is a state of mind. And so is prosperity. Think rich. Feel rich. Pamper yourself. Window-shop at the best stores. Remember, the best stores have sales too; that's the time to go *inside.* Reverend Ike said that when he was a boy he used to walk all the way

down from Harlem to the swanky Waldorf-Astoria so he "could rub elbows with them rich folks." He had the right idea. He was picking up their vibrations—vibrations of wealth, of security, of self-confidence.

Make these five guidelines part of your life . . . practice them until they are second-nature . . . and I guarantee that you will raise your prosperity consciousness and you'll be better off than you would otherwise.

CHAPTER XIII

The Job Challenge

How to Get a Better Job . . .
and How to Get Ahead Faster in it

So many people seem unhappy in their work. This is a shame considering the amount of time we have to spend at our jobs—nearly one-third of our lives or one-half of our waking time. Money is not the most important reward for our labors. We need a fair monetary reward for our services, of course, but what is far more important is the amount of satisfaction we derive from our work. Distaste for our job or boredom at it can produce insidious effects.

"How do I know if I'm in the right job?" you ask. Quite simple. Do you *enjoy* what you are doing? Do you look forward to going to your work each morning? If not, maybe you should look for another position.

"But how do I know which would be the right job for me?"

Again simple. Make a list of the ten things you enjoy doing most. Position them in order of the ones you like best.

Then study the top three occupations. These are the activities you like best. Then why not make a career out of one of them? Why not get paid for doing something you like, something you really enjoy?

Because no matter what you have written down on your list, someone is making a living out of those activities. You like eating? Some people make a living out of going to restaurants and writing their experiences for the local newspaper—and get paid for it!

Like movies? People get paid for attending films and reviewing them. No matter what activity it is, someone is making a living out of just that. And the odds are you can too!

Now of course you have to know something about that particular field. You have to master the technical details. It's no use applying for a secretarial post if you don't know typing and shorthand. You have to sharpen your professional skills for whatever posts interest you.

Even if it's being a movie reviewer. It's not just a case of going to the picture house and relaxing. You have to read and study about direction, set design, acting styles, etc. So equip yourself to qualify.

Then, "When you go fishing, go where the fish are!" Pinpoint prospective employers for your services. Remember, you only need *one.*

Do a mental affirmation that the Right Job exists *already* . . . it's just a matter of making contact with it, of attracting it into your orbit.

Prepare and send your resume, with a brief covering letter, to the prospective employers. You don't need to mail out thousands; remember you want only one job, just one button to come up bingo!

Your resume should be neatly typed, and easy to read, with wide margins. List your latest position first and then work backwards and briefly give details of your school prowess. Be succinct. Prospective employers just want the highlights. They can always ask for more details if they wish. Play up your accomplishments, but be ready to prove them. Also be specific. Don't just say "increased sales." Spell it out, "increased sales twenty percent in one year."

Wait one week and then telephone the prospective employer's secretary to find out if your letter was received and what the reaction is. Do *not* telephone and ask for the prospective employer. Ask instead for his or her secretary. The employer is a busy person and the secretary's job includes responses of the sort you seek. In fact, you may learn your letter has been forwarded to someone else—another department head may have an opening, or you may even be referred to the personnel department. The secretary can guide and advise you in regard to your follow up. In fact, secretaries can be most helpful.

Above all, hold the firm mental conviction that the right job for you, the job that will give you utmost satisfaction in every way, *exists* . . . and is waiting for you out there. You are attracting it to you, closer and closer.

Have faith, have confidence. Keep on. Be positive. That right job for *you* is coming closer.

The Job Interview

At last! You receive a phone call inviting you for an interview. Try to find out as much as you can about the company. Go to your local library, and see if the company is listed. Ask for help. Ask around. Determine if it's the type company you would enjoy working for. Does it have a good reputation? Does this company make or sell something that makes a contribution to society? Maybe it's just a small company and you won't be able to ferret out much information beforehand. But do what you can.

The night before your interview is the most important part of it! Remember how Billie Jean King prepared for her championship tennis matches by programming herself mentally in advance? That's what you're going to do. But you have the disadvantage of not being acquainted with the other player, as Billie Jean was. Never mind. You can program yourself to project an air of confidence, of sincerity, a pleasant appearance. Do this several times before you fall asleep. *Know* that if this is the right job for you, that you will then obtain the position. Visualize yourself in the interview. See yourself sitting up straight, appearing natural, putting your best *look* forward!

Do *not* visualize the other person's response. Do not project anyone hiring you.

Why not?

Because that is *black* magic. It may work, but you would pay a price for infringing on others' free will. Be content with visualizing an atmosphere of a successful outcome to the interview. Know that what is the best for all parties will come about. After all, this might not be the best job for you; then you certainly wouldn't want it. You want what's best for you. And that might just be another job entirely. So program your side of the interview and let go of the rest.

During the Interview

Naturally you're wearing your best suit or dress and presenting a smart businesslike appearance. Don't overdress but don't look sloppy either. Save your jeans for the weekend. First appearances *do* count. Make sure yours is a good one. Don't smoke—unless you're invited to. Don't chew gum. And most important, inwardly compose yourself to a calm yet alert vibration. Tell yourself inwardly, "I project confidence, sincerity, and a pleasant appearance."

Remember this: the odds are on your side. There's nothing more that the person facing you across the desk would like to do than hire you. Look at the "in" box. Note how full it is. This person would love to be able to settle one matter, that of filling the open position in order to get on with the myriad other problems awaiting attention. So everything is on your side!

For your part, you can size up your potential employer, the secretary, the office environment and the other workers. Do you like what you see?

Then absorb what you're being told about the duties of the job. If they appeal to you, then make up your mind this is the post you want.

Again, remember your prospective employer is also rooting for you. No one wants to waste fifteen minutes interviewing you without any tangible results. The interviewer *wants* you to succeed.

How to get ahead faster

Hooray! You've won the day and the job is yours. Go out and celebrate.

Now here's a surefire way to guarantee you will get ahead faster and be more successful on the job. The secret of success in business can be summed up in one word: *service.* Service, service, service. If you're a sales person, think of yourself as a *service* person. Think of how your product will benefit the prospect. Think in terms of your prospect's needs. Look at it through his or her eyes.

No matter what your occupation, tackle your job in the light of service. If you are an office worker, approach every task in the light of service. You are benefitting your company and your company's customers.

"But what if this is not appreciated?"

Ralph Waldo Emerson had the answer. "If you serve an ungrateful master, serve him all the more!" Yes, because you can't lose. The Law of Karma is on your side, working for you. What you give out is what you will get back. If you perform your duties grudgingly, with an air of resentment, you won't get very far. But put your all into your work in a constructive manner and it's *bound* to come back to your benefit. The Law of Karma is as factual a law as the law of gravity.

In business we talk about the ten percent person. The person who goes the extra mile. The person who makes that extra sales call at 5 p.m. The person who's interested in getting the job done despite the hour. The person who will call *after* the sale to see if the customer is fully satisfied. The person who can be relied upon to carry out any task thoroughly. A reliable person. These are the people for whom business is crying out. There will always be jobs for these people.

And service, because of the Law of Karma, ensures that the extra efforts you make are always rewarded. Maybe not always in the short-term, but certainly always in the long-term. In fact your reward may not be on your current job; it could consist of an offer of another job. Regardless, your attitude of service *always* pays off. Guaranteed!

Actually there is more to our daily work than meets the eye. For it provides a unique double opportunity: to be of service to the world by choosing a field that produces a worthwhile product or service—and to develop our own character inwardly by a positive attitude toward our duties. For life is all of a piece; we can't divorce our 9 to 5 activity from the rest of our experience. It has to justify itself in more than monetary terms.

I've been fortunate. I've spent most of my career in educational publishing. And that gave me the opportunity to make a contribution to the educational systems of Third World countries.

"Wait a minute," you say. "That doesn't apply to me, I just have to make a living."

Sure, but it's *how* you make a living that counts. Earlier we suggested you find work doing something you enjoy—and there must be something you enjoy doing! And at the same time why not make it count double—in a business that helps people or provides a necessary product?

And to get the most out of your work in satisfaction and achievement, put in something extra. Buddhism has a work philosophy called dharma. Basically it means that we look upon work as something more than just work, as something *higher*. For example, it is not that we work for an employer and therefore resent the time we have to give to the employer, but that we really work for ourselves. If we are a dishwasher we can determine to be the best dishwasher ever, to get those dishes sparkling, squeaky, shining. We all know how a waiter can make or mar a meal. Surly ungracious service detracts from the occasion, but a pleasant friendly helpful waiter adds much to it. Guess which waiter is happier at work? And which one gets the bigger tips!

We all know people who manage to just get by in their jobs. They do as little as possible, no more than they have to. But you can't tell me they are happy in their work. They don't derive the warm glow which stems from knowing you have done your very best. They don't go home at night feeling content about things.

In the precincts of the prestigious Englewood Club, founded in 1889, I often hear business executives complain that too few young people possess sufficient vision to focus on long range goals. "They're all after the quick buck!" "They're too impatient to reap the top rewards without being willing to work for them!"

I prize a letter from a distinguished business competitor, Harold W. McGraw, Jr., chairman of McGraw-Hill, Inc., upon my retirement, in which he writes, "You have had an outstanding publishing career which I have greatly admired, for coupled with ability, you have put in far more plain old hard work than most." Yes, there's no free lunch. And there's no substitute for hard work. Mr. McGraw and other top business leaders know that. Thomas Edison is attributed with saying that genius is one percent inspiration and ninety-nine percent perspiration!

But that hard work can be fun! It all depends on our attitude to it. Approached positively it's transformed into a rewarding and satisfying release for our energies.

"I'm just a small cog in the wheel," you complain. Small or big, every cog counts. Why, the first impression outsiders receive of a company is usually from a switchboard operator or receptionist. What a difference a friendly pleasant welcome makes!

Every person on earth ought to enjoy the sweet taste of success, to find peace and happiness, to live an interesting, secure and abundant life. It's up to us. We can if we choose. But happiness is an inside job. We all view the world from inside out. And one major avenue to happiness is finding a satisfying constructive line of work where we can give full expression to our abilities.

Therefore I hope this chapter on the Job Challenge proves helpful to you. Good luck with your own job challenge!

CHAPTER XIV

Life is a Voyage

I'm dictating this chapter on the *S.S. Oceanic*. This is a lovely ship and we are having a great time. As the prow slices through the blue waters of the Caribbean I can't help but think that life is like a voyage.

Last night we ran into some rough weather. But we felt little discomfort because this modern ship has built-in stabilizers which automatically correct any undue rolling from one side to the other. Same thing in life. We can't avoid running into rough weather from time to time, we are bound to be buffeted by the vicissitudes of life occasionally, but we too can employ our own built-in stabilizer to help correct the situation and bring ourselves back to an even equilibrium. In other words, we can't stop things happening to us, but we can control our reaction to those events. We can stabilize ourselves. We can roll with the punches.

When the captain of this liner set sail from New York he had to set a course to our destination. In fact, first, he had to know where we were going, and then work out the most direct route and the one which would consume the least fuel. Same with life. First we have to establish our destination, fix our goal in life. Then we need to chart our course to reach that goal by the most direct route as quickly as possible. If we don't have a goal in life, nothing to aim for, then we will wander aimlessly day by day just as the ship would if it had no course to adhere to.

For instance, if the liner wanted to go to Europe from New York, the captain could point it generally east and sooner or later we would land at some point in Europe. But we wouldn't know where beforehand. And it might take us weeks of zig-zagging to do so. No, the proper way is to decide first *where* we want to go, and then work out the best direct route. Likewise in life we need to decide where exactly we want to be and then work out the best way to get there. If we don't have any goals in life, then it's unlikely we will make anything of ourselves.

This morning, I thought of yet another comparison. We are all passengers on the great ship of life. We know that there has to be a captain of the ship somewhere. But just as I have not seen the captain of the *S.S. Oceanic,* so we may not see the captain of this ship of life. But we know there has to be one. You can't have a ship without a captain, and it is equally inconceivable that we could have these millions of universes without some higher directing Intelligence. And just as we have full confidence in this liner's captain, that he knows what he is doing and what the course is and will get us there safely, so we can have confidence in the Captain of the universe.

As passengers on this liner, we can either skulk down in our cabins afraid of meeting people or we can enjoy the run of the ship and take advantage of all its many attractions aboard. We can determine to make our way to the very top deck where we can enjoy the sea breeze and bask in the sunshine. The choice is ours. Down below in the scuppers in our false security, or climb the highest with many exciting adventures enroute.

CHAPTER XV

What's Your Goal?

Notice how some people drift through life, never quite making it, never amounting to anything? They just meander through each day, bounced around, grateful when they can collapse in front of their TV at night.

But *you're* different. You know what you want and how to get it. You've set your goals. Most important, you've written them down. By putting them on paper you not only are forced to clarify them in your mind, but you also are setting into motion that attraction which will draw them to you. By concentrating on your written goals over a period of time, they will inevitably and inexorably materialize in your life.

So be sure what you say you want is what you *really* want.

Everyone's heard variations of the story wherein someone is granted three wishes—and invariably uses the third and final wish to restore things to what they were before the first one.

There's a lot to be said for New Year's resolutions. They are an annual reminder that we *should* set goals, that we should try to improve the quality of our lives and uplift them, that we should strive to be better than we are. For that's what life is all about. That's why we are here.

But we don't have to wait for the New Year to form our resolutions. Every day is a new beginning, a new deal all around.

Why not *today?* Forget yesterday, and all the other yesterdays. Let them fade away. TODAY is the time to begin and NOW is the moment. The poet Goethe exclaimed, "Seize this very minute! Dare to begin and the task is half done!"

You CAN be all you wish to be. Nothing can prevent you. Life is beckoning you. Picture your goal in clear bright colors. Visualize it becoming a reality. Write it down. Capture it on paper. And then, to paraphrase Emile Coué, every day in every way, you'll be coming closer and closer to achieving your goal!"

CHAPTER XVI

ESP—How to Put
Your Mind to Work for You

"ESP," you say, "Isn't that that funny stuff, way out?"

Not at all. You've probably been using ESP yourself without realizing it! Like the character in Moliere's play *Le Bourgeois Gentilhomme* who discovered he had been speaking prose all his life without knowing it!

A number of famous people have admitted to using and following their intuition, including Winston Churchill, General Patton, Abraham Lincoln, Franklin Roosevelt, and Einstein, to mention but a few. You'd hardly consider these people flaky!

Haven't you ever had a *hunch?* Sure you have. Everyone has. Business executives talk about their *gut reactions.* Well, hunches and gut reactions are nothing more or less than ESP.

What is ESP? Extra sensory perception. Meaning something beyond our normal five senses. But how do we know we only have five senses? We may have ten—and have just not discovered the others yet. Just like electricity wasn't discovered until a couple of centuries ago yet it had been around for thousands of years.

Some people call ESP our *sixth* sense. Maybe it is. But maybe there are a few more too. Anyway, ESP is very much a part of our daily lives; maybe we just haven't been as conscious of it as we should.

Because we can put ESP to work *for* us. Many business leaders have. Conrad Hilton, for instance, wrote in his autobiography, *Be My Guest,* that whenever he had an important decision to make, sometimes involving millions of dollars, he would seek out a quiet church and go in there and sit down. This way, not only could he be away from office interruptions and telephone calls, but he could tune in to the vibrations of the thousands of churchgoers who had combined to make it a holy place. Sitting quietly, letting his mind relax, he writes that he usually had the solution to his business problem come to him—and whenever he followed his intuition it was *inevitably* right.

Conrad Hilton said, "I've been accused of playing hunches . . . I further believe most people have them, whether they follow them or not." In his opinion the key to intuition is in listening for a response. "What pushes me into action is my feeling, that go-ahead intuition that nudges me," said Hilton.

William Paley, chairman of CBS, Inc., is renowned for his ability to pick winners among the hundreds of TV shows considered annually by his network.

Harold Geneen, former chairman of ITT, said he could size up a person's character within 45 seconds.

The Wall Street Journal in its issue of November 3, 1983, reported that 31 percent of businesses rely more on intuition than research when deciding when to launch new products.

Notice how a couple who have been married many years instinctively understand each other without a word spoken.

And when you have to get up in the morning at a certain time for an important engagement, haven't you found yourself waking up automatically at the appointed time—even without the alarm clock going off?

Animals understand us without the power of speech. They instinctively recognize an animal lover, as well as people who dislike animals. Wild animals sense fear on the part of a human being.

It's a commonplace saying these days that, "I didn't like the vibes" of a person or place.

What are all these instances but—ESP! Whether we call it instinct or intuition or vibrations or hunches—they all add up to the same thing. ESP. An extra [outside] sensory perception. Of course, actually it's not outside at all, it's *inside*. It's part of the unfathomed depths of our minds. We have gone out into space exploring the universe; we have yet to explore the intricacies of our own minds and their full potential.

You've heard about left brain and right brain? How the left brain is analytical and right brain is creative? The left brain is critical while the right brain is intuitive. Too many of us have gone through life relying on our left brain; we've forgotten to make full use of our right brain.

Mental telepathy is an output of our right brain. How many times have you been thinking of someone and then the phone would ring and, yes, it would be him! We have a long way to go to understand the powers of the mind, to know how telepathy works. But I believe in it. And I'll tell you why.

Some years ago, I awoke abruptly at 1:30 in the morning. To my amazement I saw my mother standing by my bed. How could this be? My mother lived in England,

3,000 miles away. Yet, I not only *saw* my mother, I *knew* it was she. Every pup knows its mother instinctively. Yet she was dressed in the styles they wore back in the Twenties— little hats and short skirts—and I saw that her face was youthful and beautiful and unlined. Her presence was overpowering and I pinched myself to make sure I was awake.

She smiled at me, a lovely radiant smile. And then she faded away and I was left staring into the darkness, wondering, wondering.

Next morning I received a telephone call from England to tell me that my mother had died at 7:30 in the morning their time. Allowing for the six hour difference in time zones, that was exactly the minute when she appeared to me! And I realized what had happened: my mother's love had transcended physical boundaries to let me know that she was free of the body with all its aches and pains and was serenely happy.

Such is the power of love and the power of mind.

How can we put ESP to work for us? Mainly by practicing it day after day, in little ways and big. A well-known technique is to use ESP to find a parking space. Just say to yourself as you drive around the block, "I am going to come across an open parking spot for my car." And chances are you will!

Tennis is a mental game. ESP places a good player in the right position at the right time. You can use ESP to find lost articles. Just affirm, "Nothing can really be lost. It must be somewhere. My mind will direct me to it." State this firmly and let it sink into your consciousness and then dismiss it from your mind. Or better yet, affirm it just before going to sleep. Upon awakening in the morning, you should have your answer.

Poker players use ESP to sense their opponents' cards. Not that I'm recommending gambling, mind you!

Spiritual Frontiers Fellowship has an on-going program which very interestingly proves the value of ESP. It's called Blind Awareness. Under the direction of its founder, Carol Ann Liaros,[4] groups have been formed around the country to teach ESP to blind people. Through this program blind people have been taught to place their hands over colored pieces of paper and to identify the colors. But it's much more than this. Many of the blind people taking this SFF program declare it has added a new dimension to their lives. They say they are now able to cope much better with their blindness. This SFF program has been endorsed by the Lions Clubs of America who specialize in helping the blind.

Carol Ann Liaros has taken a blind student with a group of observers to a building unknown to any of them. She leads the blind person through a meditation and asks that they travel mentally upstairs and into a room on the floor above. She then asks that they describe in detail what they are "seeing." The blind person related where the position of the couch is, the color, length; the pictures on the wall, and describes what is in them, where the window is positioned, where the chairs are placed and colors in the room. Then the group goes upstairs and into the room the blind person had "seen." To the amazement of the entire group, the room is *exactly* as the person described it.

---

[4]5201 SW 22nd Terrace, Fort Lauderdale, FL 33312

We all have ESP. This power, this energy, is here, there, everywhere. Quietly invite it into your heart.

You can use ESP in daily life—sizing up people and situations, helping you make the right choices, and in many other ways. So listen to your intuition. It comes to you from that sacred place within. Like oysters, we all have within us a pearl of great price. This is our spiritual center. All that is fine and noble about us emanates from this place.

CHAPTER XVII

The Sun is Your Friend

The Egyptians and many other ancient civilizations worshipped the Sun. And with good reason. For the Sun is to our universe what our heart is to our human body. It is the spiritual window into our material world. The Sun is the closest visual approximation we have of our Creator, of That which created us and everything in the universe. Without the physical Sun, there would be no life. It supports our very existence.

And on the psychological front, too, the Sun is king. Don't we all feel better on a sunny day? Don't we talk about a sunny disposition? We even portray Old King Sol as a beaming countenance with rays in every direction.

The Egyptians visualized the sun god Ra disappearing below the horizon each evening to voyage through the underworld of night and death only to emerge triumphantly again each dawn. Some 3600 years ago the great Egyptian Pharoah Akhenaton composed a beautiful hymn to the Sun which he recited each morning. It has long been a tradition in many religions to be awake to greet the sun when it appears each morning. And I highly recommend this practice of the sunrise meditation. It enables us to tap into nature's powerful rhythm at a time when the newly stirring vibrations of daytime are building their energies. Thus we become empowered to move with their momentum to start our day.

You may feel that getting up for the sunrise each morning is a bit too early! Well of course it all depends on the time but even if it is way before your normal rising time, you can always go back to bed for another hour or so afterwards. As you practice getting up for the sunrise meditation over a period of years, you will find that something automatically awakens you before the Sun rises to allow you to be in position to greet its appearance—no matter where you may be in the world. This automatic inner alarm clock is most interesting. It is almost as though the Sun sends you a message, "I am coming. Prepare to greet me!"

So rise in time, splash water over your face, rinse your eyes, freshen up and clean your mouth. Should you not do all these things to meet your Beloved? Then sit receptively at a window facing east adopting the old Egyptian posture of sitting on a chair with hands on your knees. [Don't use the normal yogi cross-legged meditation posture here, that is where you are kindling the energies *within* yourself. Here you are trying to be receptive, to receive the energies of the dawning Sun.]

Relax and enjoy the beautiful multi-hued colors of the dawning sky. Is it not significant that we only see such beautiful colors at sunrise and sunset, not during the rest of the day? This indicates that there is something special about these two times when the currents of the earth change from night to day and day to night. The yang and yin, the polar forces of our turning globe make their cross connection and there is power, enormous power at this mystical time.

Concentrate upon the horizon. Let go of whatever personal thoughts may have crowded your mind upon awakening. This is a precious moment. Reserve your attention for the few minutes of splendor about to unfold. Soon you'll be communing with your Creator—God in all its magnificence. Keep your eyes glued upon the horizon waiting for the magical moment when you espy the first glimpse of the golden orb that signals the appearance of God, the Supreme Power, manifesting in all its majesty.

Ah, there it is! The moment has arrived. You perceive the rim of that red ball almost coyly peeking above the hills. It materializes further into its fullness. It climbs triumphantly into the sky. Its radiance is bestrewn upon all things and all living creatures. If you squint your eyes slightly you'll see its rays shining directly into your own chest, into your own physical heart—the center of your own life being. No matter how many millions of humans it shines upon, the sun has a ray for each of them.

As the sun waxes stronger you are bathed in golden splendor. Visualize its strength penetrating every atom and living cell of your body, renewing and reinvigorating and bestowing radiant health upon you. You have plugged into the God connection. Imagine it energizing every core of you. Invite this honored Guest into your soul.

As the sun climbs higher into the heavens, visualize its rays spreading out with majesty and power to embrace all humanity—and you are one with it and with all living things within it. As its light becomes stronger, protect your eyes by half closing them, and then offer up to its benediction those near and dear to you who are in need of physical or mental healing. See them enveloped within its healing light. Worship this Living Presence.

Close your meditation with a prayer for all mankind that everyone may realize the spiritual purpose of their lives, the spiritual meaning of the universe and draw closer to the Supreme Being.

Ralph Waldo Emerson said that if the stars came out but once a year, we would all rush out into the streets to marvel at them. We would all be awestruck at the impressive celestial display. What if the sun rose but once a year? Would not we treat it as the most important event in our calendar? Wouldn't we gather in the streets and on the hills and—yes, worship at this miracle? It is as close to *visually* witnessing God itself as most of us are likely to experience. The majesty, the magnificence, the overwhelming beauty of the golden sunrise!

Where possible, repeat this meditation at sunset. Here the sun's rays tend to be gentler and softer, and are most beneficial for healing purposes. Feel them penetrating you with balm-like healing power. Watch the sun disappear as it sinks below the horizon, but know that it will reappear. Its seeming death is yet another visual proof of the truth of reincarnation . . . for it will most assuredly reemerge and light up the world once again after the period of darkness.

The sunrise/sunset meditations in no way are intended as replacements for regular meditations. There is no substitute for the latter. Rather, they are complementary. You see the sunrise/sunset meditations are observing the Higher Power from a distance sending love and veneration to it. Whereas regular meditation is identifying with that Higher Power, becoming one with it. Regular meditation may be practiced before or after sunrise/sunset meditations, or at bedtime, or whenever convenient. For the best exposition of regular meditation practice, I refer the reader to *The Secret Path* Paul Brunton, a classic treatise on this subject.[5]

---

[5]Brunton: *The Secret Path,* 1985, Mountainvue Publications, distributed by Samuel Weiser, Inc., Box 612, York Beach, ME 03910.

CHAPTER XVIII

The Enchanted Cottage

Remember a movie sometime back by this title? It starred Dorothy McGuire and Robert Young. They played the parts of two hideously disfigured people who have to put up with being ostracized by the world because of their appearance. People don't like to look them in the eye, they try to avoid looking at them. But Young and McGuire meet and, guess what, they fall in love. And, here's the point, they do not see each other as disfigured. They see each other as beautiful and handsome and through the magic of movie making their faces become transformed before our eyes. It's the transforming power of love, of course.

My lovely aunt Helga, who is in her eighties, told me that inside every old person is a young person looking out.

In truth, everybody is two persons: the person on the outside and the person on the inside. The outside may not look too attractive. The face may not be that of a movie star.

Clothing may be worn. In fact, some people may look quite grunchy but we might be making too hasty a mistake if we judge them too quickly. I've learned this lesson myself the hard way. There might be gold beneath that slag heap!

As a result, I now make it a practice whenever I go to a conference to seek out the first grunch I find, and throw my arms around him or her and radiate love. I admit it hasn't always been easy! But the results have always been rewarding. I've come to know some interesting people this way. There's usually a reason for their outer appearance and once we dig beneath that we find the real person.

So, radiate love to the next grunch *you* encounter. Take a few minutes to find out what makes them tick. You'll be glad you did!

CHAPTER XIX

Everything's Coming Up Roses!

Everything's coming up roses! That is, if you've been planting roses. What's that, you say you've got quite a few *weeds* in your life experience? Then it's time to get out the weed killer. *DDT*. Destroy Dangerous Thoughts.

How do you do that? Simple. There's no room for both weeds and roses in the same spot. So deny the negative weed by jerking the thought out of your mind and flinging it far away. An effective technique to help you do this successfully is: while you're showering, as the water cascades down your body, declare forcefully that you are ridding yourself of the unwanted thought, hang-up, or whatever. Affirm "I hereby cleanse myself of all negative vibrations!" Use your hands to shake them off you.

Then, as you step out of the shower, *immediately* start planting your mental roses. Declare the opposite of the weed you have just discarded. "My body radiates with perfect health!" as you towel yourself vigorously. Or "I am bathed in the infinite peace of the Higher Power." Or "I can do all things through God who strengtheneth me!" Make whatever statement is pertinent to your particular need of the time.

Repeat this treatment daily and you'll soon notice the old negative pattern weakening as it is ousted by the new stronger positive claim. Make no mistake about it, positive overcomes negative every time, just as strength always overpowers weakness.

So turn this fact to *your* advantage! Clear out the weeds in your mental garden and replace them right away with their opposite characteristics—affirm their *positive* counterparts like a mantram. Hum it to yourself all day long for even faster results.

But how do you stop new weeds, new negatives from sprouting? After all, they're around us all the time. They're bound to creep in.

No, they are not! And here is a surefire tip to prevent weeds creeping into your consciousness. At the very first sign of a negative thought raising its ugly head, *nip it in the bud.* That's right, chop it off before it gets a chance to grow into something more serious. A good gardener is constantly on the lookout for the first shoots of a weed and then, out it comes! Keep your life sunny and bright, keep planting roses for *you!*

CHAPTER XX

Everything's All Right!

Yes, and are you ready for this—even when things *seem* to be going wrong, everything's still all right!

Oh, he's really off his rocker now, I can hear you saying. No . . . take a minute tó look at it this way. You believe in God, right? There *has* to be some higher power directing this universe.

They tell the story of Napoleon listening to the savants of the Academy Francaise trying to disprove the existence of God until, jumping to his feet, the Emperor pointed out the window to the stars and exclaimed, "That's all very well, gentlemen, but then *Who* made those?"

So if we agree that there is a Higher Intelligence behind it all, that as Shakespeare wrote, "There's a divinity that shapes our ends," then the very least we can do is give that Intelligence credit for knowing what It is doing. Sure it's difficult to comprehend God's workings; after all we are the finite trying to fathom the infinite. And that is mathematically impossible! So we have to take many things on trust, on faith, as it were. Like the little boy in Sunday school who, when his teacher asked him to define faith, replied "Believing in what ain't so!"

So when things come into your life which are not exactly what you yourself would have ordered from the menu, take a moment to ask, "Why?" Try to search back for the roots of the problem, don't judge it by surface appearance. Ask, "Why has this happened to me?" If you are strictly honest with yourself, you may be about to discern the *real* causes and surprise! Guess *who* is responsible? That's right, our chickens have come home to roost every time. It is like a boomerang. What we throw out the world sooner or later returns to us—for better or worse. Our actions, even our thoughts, are hostages to fate.

That's what it's all about. The carousel of life. But here's the good news! There has to be a meaning to all this, there's a reason for it. And that reason now seems very obvious. The Higher Intelligence is allowing us to learn from our mistakes. A child doesn't stick a finger in the fire twice. So here we are, in the nursery of life, getting knocked about a bit, true—but we are being educated by our experiences. We are given the option to choose our experiences—we ourselves press the buttons marked "Good" and "Bad."

That's why when we've pressed the wrong button and we have to suffer the penalty, *it's still all right*—we are learning which button to press next time. Meanwhile, our unpleasant experiences, these too shall pass. And they will pass all the sooner if we focus our attention on the *right* button. Don't make the same mistake twice. So it's really all right, after all. No matter what happens, it's really all right.

As the poet Robert Browning declared, "God's in his heaven, all's right with the world."

CHAPTER XXI

Accentuate the Positive!

"Accentuate the positive, eliminate the negative . . ." Remember that old Bing Crosby ballad? Whether he knew it or not, the crooner was expressing a great metaphysical truth. Simply put, we can't have two contrasting thoughts at the same time. If we're holding a positive thought, then there's no room for a negative thought.

This truth opens great possibilities for us. Think of your mind as a garden plot. There's only so much room for anything to grow. If we fill our plot with positive flowers, there won't be room for any negative weeds.

The more we plant positive seeds in our mind, the less opportunity there is for negatives to take over. More and more positive seeds create more and more positive flowers. Soon they will crowd out any negative weeds. And our garden of the mind will be a lovely bouquet of flowers.

How do we do this, you ask? Easy. Here's a simple technique. The moment a negative seeks admission to your mind follow the advice of the song and *eliminate* it. Nip it in the bud. It's a lot easier to do when it's small; much harder if we let it grow into a sturdy bush.

And the most effective way to overcome a negative intruder is to supplant it *immediately* with its opposite. Form a good strong mental picture of its positive obverse and let it sink in. Remember, there's only room for one thought at a time. That's the key to successful control of our minds. Negatives cannot storm our defenses in an overwhelming mass; they can only enter one at a time. That makes it much easier to knock them off as they come in the door.

Let's try it out. Feel *angry?* OK, what's the opposite of anger? That's right, love. So zap that angry thought by implanting a *big love thought.* There isn't room for two thoughts . . . so love takes over and drives out anger.

Impatient? Force yourself to relax by musing on the unhurried movements of the stars and planets in their orbits—slowly, surely, steadily running their courses as though they have all eternity. For they do . . . and so do we.

Afraid? Innoculate yourself with a powerful injection of faith. That which created us is always with us, ready to support us with Its love. Turn to the Higher Power and absorb Its strength. Your fears will fade like chimeras in the sunlight.

So always reach for the antidote whenever a negative tries to penetrate your consciousness. Eliminate it by accentuating the positive!

CHAPTER XXII

Where's Your Consciousness?

Remember the newspaper story of the old lady who passed away in a small room in a run-down section? How she had lived in squalor for many years, subsisting on canned food, wearing old clothes. Yet they discovered hundreds of thousands of dollars under her mattress! Yes, she had lived as though she were poor . . . yet actually she was rich!

But, despite all her money, was she really rich or was she poor? Right, she was poor because she lived poor. She created her own world of scarcity even when there was none.

How many of us are like that? Maybe not to that extreme . . . but some of us do accept the delusion of scarcity in a world of abundance. Because God *is* abundance. It has to be. It can't be anything else. Can the Infinite be limited in any way? And the Infinite created us and our universe. We were created by Abundance. So how can we be anything else?

Look around you at the fantastic variety of life which this abundance has made—in vegetation, animals, insects, flowers, trees, even humans. No stinting here. Just a tremendous outpouring of everything. So how can we delude ourselves into accepting shortages? Are we like the old lady denying our abundance and settling for poverty because that was where her consciousness chose to be?

Flamboyant producer Mike Todd once said "I've been rich and I've been poor. Rich is better." He *knew* that we have a choice, that we *can* determine the quality of our lives. Because where we place our consciousness is what we attract into our lives. Reverend Ike says "Think rich." The old lady thought poor and that's what she got.

The moral is clear. Accept your abundance. Invite it into your life. Make sure you're not hiding it under the mattress. Follow Reverend Ike's example and *think prosperity*. Think rich. Think good. Follow St. Paul's advice. "All that is true, all that is seemly, all that is just, all that is pure, all that is lovable, all that is winning—whatever is virtuous or praiseworthy—let such things fill your thoughts." You'll be glad you did!

CHAPTER XXIII

The Heart Attack
as Transformer

My heart attack some years ago was the best thing that ever happened to me! When admitted to the hospital I relaxed completely; for the first time in many years I had no schedules to meet and nowhere to go and nothing to worry about. I felt a deep sense of love for the skilled nurses in the Coronary Care Unit who did such a marvelous job of caring for me.

However, I think it would be helpful if hospitals handed coronary patients a mimeographed sheet explaining what has happened, and explaining the importance of the patient's mental attitude in wanting to get well. The patient should be made aware of the wonderful repair mechanisms operating in the body and be encouraged to cooperate with them.

They say there are no atheists in a fox hole; certainly there are none in CCU. We realize that the final answer to survival is in the hands of something Greater than ourselves. And we become aware of that Higher Intelligence ("God," or what we will) which directs the living miracle of our bodies, as well as everything else in and around us.

I came out of the hospital at Easter and the date had great significance for me. I was keenly aware of the miracle of spring outside my windows and felt that I too was experiencing a rebirth. Since then life has been infinitely precious, and with renewed energy I have tried to devote it to helping others in a constructive way. I am grateful to my heart attack for opening up new vistas for progressive living.

Later I learned that ancient Hindu philosophy regards a heart attack as untieing the proverbial "knot of ignorance." They call it *granthi.* So, taken in the right way, such a seemingly negative occurrence can be a spiritual blessing in disguise. It unties the knot of ignorance and enables us to see the higher side of life. Everything happens for the best—if we *make* it happen for the best!

CHAPTER XXIV

10 Ways to Have a Great Day!

The first hour can determine the whole tenor of your day. Get off to a good start, and you'll carry the momentum with you. Try to include a meditation, if you can—preferably at sunrise when you can tap into Nature's powerful rhythm. Here are ten easy affirmations to help you tune up your mental attitude to attract only the *best* each and every day.

1) Declare out loud, "This is the day the Lord has made. I will rejoice and be glad in it!"

2) As you shower, affirm "The perfect life of God flows through me, cleansing every cell and fiber of my body, making me whole and filled with energy."

3) Resist wasting your mental power on gripes and post-mortems. Instead start thinking about

what to do *now*. Amazing things happen when you think constructively.

4) As you towel yourself dry, articulate these words aloud: "I can do all things through the Higher Power which lends me strength."

5) Upon leaving your home or apartment, as you close the door, envision a white light surrounding the entire premises. Imagine this light to be a protective barrier to keep out evil. This is more effective than any burglar alarm system!

6) As you start your car visualize a white bubble encapsulating it. No danger can penetrate the bubble. No other car can come within it to hit you. You and the car are perfectly safe. Then imagine this white light, like a thick cloud, penetrating all the moving parts of your car and ensuring their smooth safe function.

7) As you drive along say out loud with gusto, "I feel WONDERFUL!" Repeat several times until you feel enthusiasm for the day tingling through your veins.

8) Say, "Good Morning," to the cells in your body. Play some lively music for them; this stimulates them. Start at your feet and move your attention up slowly through your body, blessing every cell and organ. Feel the life force moving upwards and out through the top of your head. Breathe deeply as you do.

9) Declare "I hereby affirm that all the new cells born in this physical body during the next twenty-four hours are perfect cells—even if the cells which they replaced may have been *diseased* in any way, shape, or form. The new ones are perfect. And so it is!"

10) "I hereby affirm that if there be any shadows on my etheric body which could in any way manifest adversely onto my physical body, that they are hereby eliminated forthwith. So be it!"

Practice the above daily . . . and you'll arrive at your office refreshed, with renewed energy, eager to *have a good day!*

CHAPTER XXV

Good Morning Affirmations

Since the preceding chapter, "Ten Ways to Have a Great Day" was first published in the Spiritual Frontiers Fellowship newsletter, several people tell me they have pasted it on their bathroom mirrors. The other day one of them asked me, "What do you have on *your* bathroom mirror?"

That's a fair question. And it so happens that I do have a clipping pasted to the back of my bathroom cabinet door. Affirming it is part of my morning shaving routine.

It appeared in an article by Dr. Donald Curtis in *Science of Mind* magazine.[6] I recommend it especially to anyone in the business world.

---

[6]Readers interested in *Science of Mind* magazine subscriptions can write Box 75127, Los Angeles, 90075.

I move serenely forward into the adventure of life today. I am filled with inspiration and enthusiasm. I am guided and protected by the Infinite Intelligence. I express this Intelligence in everything I say and do. I project confidence and authority. I am sure of myself in every situation. I am filled with the strength and energy to be what I am and to do what I have to do.

Declare this out loud every morning and it becomes part of your consciousness to carry you forward into the day.

CHAPTER XXVI

Good Night Affirmations

We have discussed the visualization exercises to be done in bed before going to sleep.

Then ask your Higher Self to guide you through dreams with any problems you may have. Keep a pencil and pad near by to jot down the dream as you recall it upon awakening. If you can't understand it, ask for clarification the next night and the dream message will be given you in another way.

Now relax. As Ralph Waldo Emerson said, "Finish every day and be done with it. You have done what you could. Some blunders and absurdities no doubt crept in; forget them as soon as you can. Tomorrow is a new day; begin it well and serenely and with too high a spirit to be cumbered with your old nonsense."

I like to round out the day by saying to myself as I turn out the lights that lovely prayer of Gene Emmet Clark's:

My sleep, God-given, shall be sweet.

I forgive myself and all in my environment, and let the deep sleep of this night erase all hurt and all condemnation.

Sleep heals. And as I lie in rest there is a gathering up and a knitting together not only of the best resources of my body but also of my mind and life and spirit. Tomorrow I shall wake refreshed and I shall eagerly anticipate the day with strength and competence and happiness!

CHAPTER XXVII

Recommended Reading

A few months ago I was giving a workshop at a Spiritual Frontiers Fellowship retreat when someone asked me, "Which book do you get all your ideas from? I'd like to buy it."

I had to explain that there was no one such book which encompassed all principles which I was discussing. On the other hand, there is no new Truth—only new versions of the same Truth. None of the ideas in this book are new. I did not originate them. I have read extensively for more than fifty years, and have had the good fortune to learn from many people who have been my teachers over the years. But I can definitely avow that every single principle expressed in this book has been tried and tested and put into practice successfully by me. I absolutely can *guarantee that these principles work; they have in my* life and they will in *yours.*

Now I feel the inner prompting to pass on these principles. In fact, it's a spiritual law that one must pass on what one receives. Otherwise it's like being handed a candle in a dark room—and blowing the candle out! And so, dear reader, I pass on my candle to you . . . .

Some of the books I have found extremely useful and which I can recommend wholeheartedly to you are:

The Secret Path by Dr. Paul Brunton (Mountainvue Publications, distributed by Samuel Weiser, Inc., York Beach, ME). A classic, easy-to-follow guide to meditation, beautifully written.

The Power of Positive Thinking by Dr. Norman Vincent Peale (Prentice-Hall Inc., Englewood Cliffs, NJ) The granddaddy of all positive thinking books which has sold over four million copies. Still a mine of valuable ideas.

Emerson's Essays, (Harper and Row, NY). America's own spiritual genius.

The Power of Decision by Dr. Raymond Charles Barker (Dodd, Mead & Co., NY). The well known Science of Mind minister provides commonsense advice to help people clarify their thinking and make correct decisions.

Christian Victory Instruction by Dr. W. Frederic Keeler (Willing Publishing Co., San Gabriel, CA). Much broader than its title implies, this is an excellent treatise on mind mastery.

The Secret of Instantaneous Healing by Harry Douglas Smith (Parker Publishing Co., West Nyack, NY) If faulty emotional thinking makes us sick, then we can reverse our habits to regain healthy living. The best and most practical book I have read on this subject.

Don't Just Stand There—Live!, by Dr. G. Eric Pace (Harper & Row, NY). This popular minister writes entertainingly of applications of the law of mind.

Food, Mind and Mood, by Michael Schachter, M.D., and David Scheinkin, M.D. (Warner Books, NY). An informative guide to holistic medicine and nutrition. We are what we eat!

Numerology and the Divine Triangle, Faith Javane and Dusty Bunker (Para Research, Rockport, MA). I like this book not only for what it taught me about numerology which I find a very practical science, but also for its spiritual overtones. I can also recommend all of Dusty Bunker's subsequent books by the same publisher.

Sybil Leek's Astrological Guide by Sybil Leek (Prentice Hall, Inc. Englewood Cliffs, NJ). A basic roundup of the zodiac signs and their application to various aspects of our lives.

The Practice of the Presence of God by Brother Lawrence (Peter Pauper Press, Mount Vernon, NY). This enduring classic by the little monk is just as practicable to today's Madison Avenue.

I could list many more books which have afforded me instruction and enjoyment over the years but this selection is a good beginning for anyone. I have enjoyed browsing through my bookshelves and picking them out!

Epilogue

Now we come to the end of this book. In it I have tried to describe and explain as simply as possible the mental principles which are available to everyone in living life *purposefully*. By so doing we can take control of our lives. And this will lead us to greater heights of happiness, success and prosperity. These principles have worked for me. I have tested them all and proven them. They can work for *you* also.

More than that, they can lift your life from being a mere aimless meandering to an exciting adventure. This is the challenge.

And they can clear the way for our embarking upon an even higher quest, the spiritual quest for which we were born, namely to reunite ourselves with That which created us, to align ourselves with the Divine Spark within each of us and to see life from the highest vantage point.

All the Very BEST to You who read these lines!